THE BAD BUG BOOK
(And other annoying pests)

Insect, rodents, and other animals come in many different shapes and sizes.

But when these curious creatures invade our homes, cause damage,

or spread disease, we call them . . . PESTS

This book is all about . . .

Sneaky stingers, creepy crawlers, biting buggers, ruthless rodents, freaky flyers, and pests of all sizes.

To order additional copies of this book, contact:
Xlibris
844-714-8691
www.Xlibris.com
Orders Xlibris.com

ISBN: Softcover   978-1-4500-4067-9
         Hardcover   978-1-4500-4068-6

Library of Congress Control Number: 2010901746

Print information available on the last page

Rev. date: 09/01/2021

As a pest control technician in New York City,

I am often asked by my daughter, to explain:

why some bugs are good, and some bugs are bad.

And so . . . is the inspiration for this book.

This book is dedicated to my angel, Amanda lee

Daddy loves you.

Ants will always work together,
But do not like the rainy weather.
A picnic is their favorite site,
So check your sandwich before you bite.

Andy the Ant

Bats can be a scary sight,
and take flight, late at night.
They may bite you very quick,
And that might make you really sick.

Benny the Bat

Bed Bugs hide far out of sight,
Come out and bite us late at night.
They bite your butt, then crawl away,
In hopes to bite another day.

Barney the Bed Bug

4

Bees will buzz, and fly around,
And some of them live in the ground.
Some help the flowers, in the spring,
But you won't like them, if they sting

Betsy the Bee

5

Of all the insects, near and far,
Almost half, beetles are.
They might infest almost anywhere,
Except with fish, or polar bears.

Bobby the Beetle

Centipedes have lots of feet,
And even good bugs, they like to eat.
They love the moisture, and usually hide,
In dirt, under rocks, and even inside.

Cynthia the Centipede

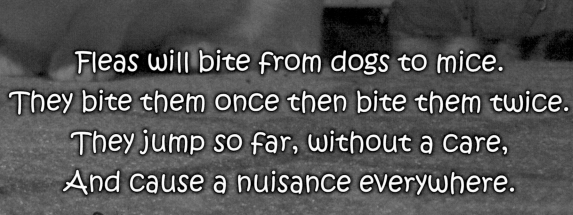

Fleas will bite from dogs to mice.
They bite them once then bite them twice.
They jump so far, without a care,
And cause a nuisance everywhere.

Frankie the Flea

Flies aren't welcome, not at all.
But are usually found on the wall.
They eat the garbage, and even poop,
Then try to swim in your soup.

Fran the Fly

Mice will stay out of sight,
And usually eat, late at night.
They raid the kitchen when they come,
And will not care to save you some.

Monte the Mouse

Mites are small and hard to see,
Some feed on dogs, mice, leaves or bees.
They hide so well, almost anywhere,
They might be hiding in your chair.

Morris the Mite

Mosquito bites can really itch,
They'll even bite you if your rich.
Stagnant water is where they breed,
And on our skin, is where they feed.

Murphy the Mosquito

Moths will feed on cloth or grain,
And they can be quite the pain.
They love the lights, and love to fly,
But they're quite annoying by and by.

Marty the Moth

Pigeons like to fly around,
And can be found all over town.
They love it when you feed them bread,
But they just might poop on your head.

Peggy the Pigeon

Possums like to creep and crawl,
And like the darkness most of all.
They like our meat, fruit, and bread,
And when they're scared, they play dead.

Peter the Possum

Raccoons are stirring while we sleep,
And in your home, they may creep.
They take our food, and then go home,
To feed their faces all alone

Randy the Raccoon

Rats will often look like mice,
But they're at least twice the size
They eat, they poop, and spread disease,
And always like a piece of cheese.

Richie the Rat

Roaches come in big and small
And in your food, they just may crawl.
They might eat grease and also grime,
And even the cat food, from time to time.

Rafael the Roach

Silverfish don't swim at all,
Instead they crawl upon your wall.
They might eat paper, sugar, hair,
And they can pop up anywhere.

Scotty the Silverfish

Spiders like to hang around,
They catch a bug, and scoff it down.
Their webs are pretty, some would say,
While other folks might run away.

Sammy the Spider

Squirrels love to run around,
And in your home they can be found.
They feed on nuts and other grain,
But they can be quite a pain.

Suzy the Squirrel

When termites come, they're not alone,
They eat you out of house and home.
They eat the beams, the floor, the chair,
They eat any wood, anywhere.

Tony the Termite

Printed in the United States
by Baker & Taylor Publisher Services